AUTONOMOUS
VEHICLES

AUTONOMOUS VEHICLES

ODYSSEYS

JIM WHITING

CREATIVE EDUCATION · CREATIVE PAPERBACKS

Published by Creative Education and Creative Paperbacks
P.O. Box 227, Mankato, Minnesota 56002
Creative Education and Creative Paperbacks are imprints of
The Creative Company
www.thecreativecompany.us

Design by Blue Design (www.bluedes.com)
Production by Colin O'Dea
Art direction by Rita Marshall
Printed in the United States of America

Photographs by Alamy (Christian Lademann/lamapress, Jim
West, Vaughn Youtz/ZUMA), Creative Commons Wikimedia
(Bettmann/Corbis/New York Times, CSIRO/Science Image,
Diablanco, Firefly4342, Steve Jurvetson/Flickr, Kivaan,
Photographer's Mate 2nd Class Daniel J. McLain/U.S. Navy,
Office of Naval Research/Flickr, Spaceape), Getty Images
(Bettmann, Bloomberg, Shoji Fujita/Taxi, mevans/E+),
iStockphoto (Arndt_Vladimir, c1a1p1c1o1m1, Chesky_W,
dszc, IGphotography, jamesteohart, scalatore1959, simonkr,
UmbertoPantalone), Shutterstock (Scharfsinn, turtix)

Library of Congress Cataloging-in-Publication Data
Names: Whiting, Jim, author.
Title: Autonomous vehicles / Jim Whiting.
Series: Odysseys in technology.
Includes bibliographical references and index.
Summary: An in-depth survey of autonomous vehicles,
examining the past, present, and future of the technological
developments, scientific principles, and innovators behind
driverless vehicles.
Identifiers: ISBN 978-1-64026-235-5 (hardcover) / ISBN 978-1-
62832-798-4 (pbk) / ISBN 978-1-64000-370-5 (eBook)

This title has been submitted for CIP processing under LCCN
2019938246.

First Edition HC 9 8 7 6 5 4 3 2 1
First Edition PBK 9 8 7 6 5 4 3 2 1

CONTENTS

Introduction

In 2002, the Defense Advanced Research Projects Agency (DARPA) announced the Grand Challenge, a contest that tasked participants with creating an **autonomous** vehicle. The ultimate goal of the competition was to protect American troops by eliminating the need for soldiers to drive in high-risk operations or unpredictable situations. Entrants had to develop a vehicle capable of traveling entirely on its own across

OPPOSITE: None of the entrants in the original Grand Challenge completed the course, but they inspired future innovations in self-driving vehicles.

OPPOSITE Stanford University's *Stanley* took home the $2 million prize for the second Grand Challenge, held in 2005.

the Mojave Desert from Barstow, California, to Primm, Nevada, in less than 10 hours. The 142-mile (229 km) course was deliberately rugged to simulate battlefield conditions.

As the sun rose on March 13, 2004, 15 vehicles left the starting line. Most quickly encountered mechanical problems. The last one broke down after just 7.5 miles (12.1 km). But DARPA regarded what seemed to be a dismal failure in a positive light. "That first competition created a community of innovators, engineers, students, programmers, off-road racers, backyard mechanics, inventors, and dreamers who came together to make history by trying to solve a tough technical problem," said a DARPA spokesperson 10 years later. Their ideas and innovations led to major advances in autonomous vehicles. Self-driving cars were on their way.

Dreaming Driverless

People were thinking about self-driving cars long before the DARPA-sponsored race. Inventor Francis P. Houdina sent a driverless car called *American Wonder* through the streets of New York City in 1925. A crew in a follow car controlled the driverless vehicle with radio signals, making it seem "as if a **phantom** hand were at the wheel," according to the *New York Times*. Similar demonstrations took place in Milwaukee, Wisconsin,

OPPOSITE: Once the dream of science fiction, autonomous vehicle technology—such as improved cruise control and driving assist components—is gradually becoming part of society.

13

the following year and in Fredericksburg, Virginia, in 1932. "The driverless car will travel about the city through the heaviest traffic, stopping, starting, turning, sounding its horn, and proceeding just as though there were an invisible driver at the wheel," gushed the Fredericksburg *Free Lance-Star* newspaper. Events such as these encouraged people to dream driverless. Science-fiction author David H. Keller wrote a short story entitled "The Living Machine" in 1935. In it, cars respond to spoken commands: "The blind for the first time were safe. Parents found they could more safely send their children to school in the new car than in the old cars with a chauffeur [driver]."

General Motors presented a scale model of a futuristic city in its Futurama exhibit at the 1939 World's Fair in New York City. It featured driverless cars and

It's Magic!

To many people, Francis Houdina's driverless car seemed almost magical. So it was a natural step to associate Houdina with the famed magician Harry Houdini (pictured). Houdini wasn't pleased, especially when he learned that some of his mail was being delivered to Houdina in error. He thought that Houdina was taking advantage of their similar names. One day the angry magician burst into Houdina's office. He accused the carmaker of using his name "unlawfully in the conduct of their business." Houdini then began throwing punches. When Houdina employees tried to restrain him, he smashed an electric chandelier with a chair. He was charged with disorderly conduct and property destruction. The charges were dropped when no one from Houdina's office showed up in court.

BELOW New York City's Futurama scale model included more than 500,000 buildings and 50,000 cars, many of which actually "drove" within the exhibit.

emphasized the safety and convenience of the automated system. "These cars ... and the highways on which they drive will have in them devices which will correct the faults of human beings as drivers," said exhibit designer Norman Bel Geddes. "They will prevent the driver from committing errors." There was good reason for this assurance. In 1900, just 36 people died in automobile accidents on American highways. By 1939, the number of fatalities had soared to more than 30,000. GM predicted that the automated system would be fully operational by 1960. It wasn't.

The 1980s marked the beginning of a surge in research surrounding self-driving cars. In 1984, researchers at Carnegie Mellon University (CMU) in Pittsburgh, Pennsylvania, built a large robot they nicknamed "Terregator" (short for Terrestrial Navigator). Terregator was capable of moving along at a top speed of 4.8 miles (7.7 km) per hour. On one occasion, it thought a nearby tree was part of the path it was following. The robotic vehicle veered off-course and climbed the tree, chewing up bark in the process. Still, as project director William "Red" Whittaker pointed out, "At a time when thinking machines were the stuff of fiction, Terregator took autonomous driving from fantasy to fact. CMU had developed the underpinnings of autonomous driving and cast that into the world."

Two years later, CMU built an improved vehicle. NavLab (short for Navigation Laboratory) was a big, blue van packed with cameras, sensors, and computers that controlled most of its functions. It also carried up to four researchers at a time. It reached a top speed of 20 miles (32.3 km) per hour. More versions of NavLab vehicles followed. Perhaps the most successful was NavLab 5. Two CMU researchers, Dean Pomerleau and Todd Jochem, took the minivan from Pittsburgh to San Diego, California, in July 1995. Although it didn't control the gas or brake pedals, the on-board computer steered for nearly the entire distance.

The DARPA Grand Challenge was the next major step. With a $1 million prize on the line, many entrants were researchers from colleges or universities who had paired up with large corporations. Others represented major carmakers such as Toyota. Southern California's Palos Verdes High School even had a team. CMU's vehicle made it the farthest before getting stuck on a hairpin turn, but no one won the race.

DARPA followed up with a second Grand Challenge on October 8, 2005. The 132-mile (212 km) course started

and finished near Primm. This time, the prize was $2 million. The second challenge was far more successful than the first. All but 1 of the 23 teams went beyond the previous year's farthest mark. Five vehicles finished the course. The winning team was from Stanford University. Its vehicle finished in 6 hours and 54 minutes, with an average speed of 19.1 miles (30.7 km) per hour. Teams from CMU placed second (7 hours and 5 minutes) and third (7 hours and 14 minutes). TerraMax, a 15-ton (13.6 t) behemoth from Wisconsin's Oshkosh Truck Corporation and its partners, was the final finisher, though its time of 12 hours and 51 minutes was well past the 10-hour deadline.

In 2007, DARPA offered the Urban Challenge. Driverless cars had to maneuver through a complex 55-mile (88.5 km) course at an abandoned air force base near Victorville, California. It was a small community, complete with office buildings, homes, streets, and parking lots. Six of the 11 teams completed the course, and a CMU team won the $2 million prize. Its vehicle averaged about 14 miles (22.5 km) per hour. "The real winner was technology," said DARPA director Tony Tether. Someone asked him when DARPA would stage another challenge. "There won't be one," he replied. "Mission accomplished."

The publicity the DARPA contests generated within the technology community had profound effects. Sebastian Thrun, one of the leaders of the Stanford team that won the second Grand Challenge, soon received unexpected visitors: Larry Page and Sergey Brin, cofounders of the tech giant Google. They had lots of questions. Thrun's answers helped persuade

Within a few years, Google's autonomous cars had traveled more than 300,000 miles (482,803 km).

Page and Brin to enter the self-driving field. Within a few years, Google's autonomous cars had traveled more than 300,000 miles (482,803 km). In 2016, the Google unit that produced self-driving cars became a separate company called Waymo.

Brin and Page aren't the only tech titans in the field. Entrepreneur Elon Musk, who founded the electric car company Tesla, also turned his attention to self-driving cars. "I think [autonomous driving]'s just going to become normal. Like an elevator," Musk said in 2015. "They used to have elevator operators, and then we developed some simple circuitry to have elevators just come to the

What's in a Name?

In 1997, Sergey Brin and Larry Page wanted a different name for their new search engine. Fellow Stanford student Sean Anderson suggested googolplex. Page shortened it to googol. The word *googol* dates back to 1920. Mathematician Edward Kasner wanted a fun name to describe the number 1 followed by 100 zeroes. His nine-year-old nephew Milton suggested *googol*. Then Milton came up with *googolplex*, which he defined as "one, followed by writing zeroes until you get tired." More formally, it is a number so large that it could never be fully written out. Anderson checked the **Internet domain name registry** to see if googol .com was available. He mistakenly typed google.com. That was available, so Page registered it. The company was formally incorporated in 1998.

floor that you're at—you just press the button."

By then, many major carmakers and startup companies had gotten into the autonomous act. In 2013, a self-driving car from Italian-based VisLab successfully negotiated an eight-mile (12.9 km) course through the crowded, twisting city streets of Parma, Italy. The following year, an Audi driverless car acting entirely on its own reached speeds of 149 miles (240 km) per hour on a German racetrack. Two years later, an Audi traveled from San Francisco, California, to Las Vegas, Nevada, a distance of about 560 miles (901 km). It covered nearly the entire distance on its own, though a driver took the wheel in urban areas.

The race is on. Many people believe that it is only a matter of time before U.S. highways and city streets are filled with self-driving cars.

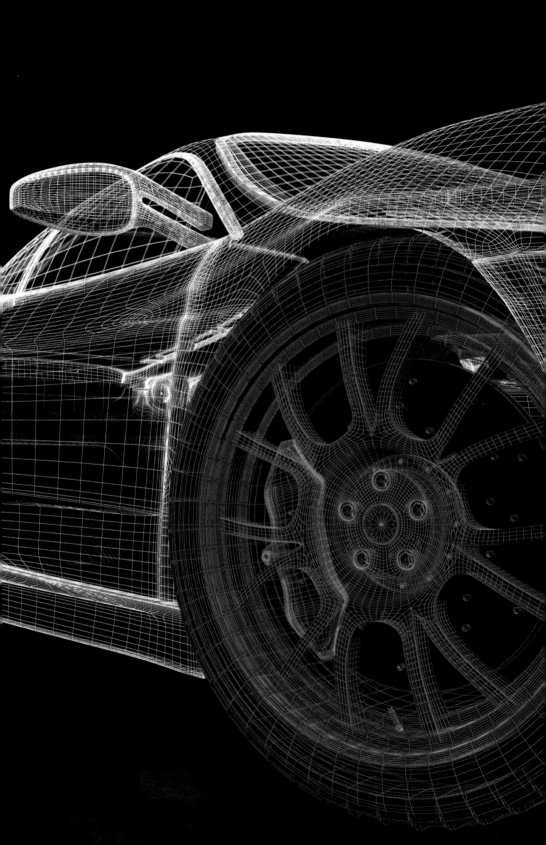

Autonomous Function

Regardless of approach, all companies that are developing self-driving cars utilize artificial intelligence (AI). The term "artificial intelligence" was first used by computer scientist John McCarthy in a paper written in 1955. He wanted to clarify and develop concepts surrounding so-called "thinking machines." In its most basic form, AI refers to the ability of computers or computer-controlled

OPPOSITE: Researchers believe that the use of driverless vehicles will reduce the number of fatalities on roadways each year.

devices (such as robots or self-driving cars) to simulate human thinking.

AI has two forms. Narrow, or "weak," AI has the ability to perform a single task. This form has been in common use in the automobile industry for years. One example is anti-lock braking systems (ABS). Increasingly available throughout the 1970s, ABS are now standard on most vehicles. When a driver applies the brakes, the ABS instantly determines if one or more wheels is locking up. If that happens, the car could go into a skid and crash. To prevent that, a series of valves reduces the braking on the wheels, pumping the brakes up to 15 times per second, and thereby allowing the driver to maintain control. Weak AI also appears in the form of Amazon .com recommendations and Google search suggestions that pop up after a person types just a few letters.

Look, Ma, No Hands!

On July 23, 1995, Carnegie Mellon researchers Dean Pomerleau and Todd Jochem set out in a Pontiac minivan from Pittsburgh on a cross-country trek. The third team member was a computer program called RALPH (Rapidly Adapting Lateral Position Handler). RALPH did almost all the driving on freeways. It took pictures of the road ahead to produce steering commands that kept the car in its lane. Pomerleau and Jochem controlled the gas pedal and brakes and took over on surface streets. They arrived in San Diego, California, seven days later. RALPH drove nearly 3,000 miles (4,828 km). They called their trip "No Hands Across America."

General, or "strong," AI is designed to mimic human intelligence and provide solutions to unfamiliar tasks. In self-driving cars, AI must deal with countless driving situations. As self-driving pioneer William Whittaker points out, "You can't program a car for every imaginable situation, so at some stage, you have to trust that it will cope with just about anything that's thrown at it, using whatever intelligence it has. And it's hard to be confident about that, especially when even the smallest misunderstanding, like mistaking a paper bag for a large rock, could lead a car to do something unnecessarily dangerous." Instead of programming autonomous vehicles for a variety of circumstances, engineers focused on a single prediction problem: What would a human do? "The reason AI works so well in a self-driving car ... is that we have thousands of measurements in real time in the form of embedded sensors all around the car and in the environment," explains technologist and inventor Amir Husain.

But even after driving millions of miles, the AI in self-driving cars still hasn't experienced all the potential situations that it could possibly encounter. So it hasn't developed solutions to those issues, either. This could prove problematic during the period in which some vehicles are operating autonomously while others are not. Human behavior can be unpredictable. While a self-driving car is programmed to stop at a red light, a human driver may not obey it.

Self-driving cars rely on a variety of embedded sensors to provide data about their environment to an on-board computer. Cameras provide real-time information about

what lies in front of the vehicle, such as lane lines, traffic lights, and road signs. As they improve, these cameras will recognize more aspects of the car's environment and navigate the vehicle accordingly. Autonomous vehicles also use radar. The radar unit is especially useful at detecting objects, such as cyclists or other vehicles, and determining their speed and direction. The cars also use a Global Positioning System (GPS) to establish their exact location and route.

Another tool is lidar (light detection and ranging), which is similar to radar. A sensor emits pulsed laser beams every second. It then calculates how long it takes for the beams to bounce back. That data enables the vehicle to construct a three-dimensional map that is more detailed and reliable than the two-dimensional images the cameras provide. Lidar was first used in the 1960s to map clouds. Then, in 1971, the crew of Apollo 15 used lidar to map the moon's surface. As autonomous

Thinking Big

Elon Musk (pictured, right) was born in South Africa in 1971. He taught himself computer programming when he was 10. Seven years later, he moved to Canada to attend college. He entered Stanford University in 1994. But he left two days later. He could see how important the Internet was going to become. Musk soon cofounded Zip2. It provided online maps and business directories. In 1999, he cofounded X.com, which eventually became PayPal. Musk sold both companies and became a multimillionaire. He then founded SpaceX to try to find ways of traveling to space that weren't so expensive. In 2008, one of his rockets became the first privately financed vehicle to put a satellite in Earth's orbit.

White and other lighter colors are more reflective and therefore easier to detect by lidar.

vehicles become more prevalent, lidar may even play a role in determining the color of cars. White and other lighter colors are more reflective and therefore easier to detect by lidar.

The auto industry uses the levels of driving automation determined by the Society of Automotive Engineers (SAE) International to label the degree of autonomy that cars possess:

Level 0: No autonomy. The human driver performs all driving tasks. Support features may provide warnings—such as blind-spot or lane-departure warnings—but don't take corrective measures.

Level 1: Limited driver assistance. Advanced Driver

Assistance System (ADAS) can help the driver with either steering or braking/accelerating, but not both at the same time.

Level 2: Partial automation. The vehicle can control both steering and braking/acceleration at the same time. The human driver must continue to pay full attention to his/her environment and perform the driving tasks.

Level 3: Conditional automation. The Automated Driving System (ADS) on the vehicle lets it perform all tasks under some conditions, such as driving on divided highways. The driver must resume control if conditions exceed the capability of the automated system, such as urban settings with high traffic volume.

Level 4: High automation. ADS allows the vehicle to perform all driving functions under most circumstances. Drivers may still need to step in under certain conditions.

Level 5: Fully autonomous. ADS allows the vehicle to do all the driving in all circumstances after the destination has been set. There is no need for mechanical controls, such as gas pedals and steering wheels. People in the car are only passengers and are never involved in the actual operation of the vehicle.

Vehicles being tested at Level 5 will not be available to the general public for some time, but there is little question that the process is well in motion. It may not be too much longer before people will sit in cars with comfortable chairs with refreshments in front of them while they read, play computer games, carry on conversations, or just take in the scenery around them without any concerns about staying alert to the flow of traffic.

Market on Wheels

In the spring of 2019, California-based startup Robomart launched a grocery service. It featured driverless vans carrying items such as fruit, vegetables, and even hot meals. The vehicles are electric-powered and remotely controlled using a variety of navigation tools. Customers summon the vehicles with an app and pay through their accounts. Robomart CEO Ali Ahmed calls it a "grocery store on wheels." She adds, "You don't have to spend time ordering online and you get to pick out food yourself.... We're more convenient and we carry a lot more than a vending machine, but less than a standard convenience store." **Advocates** call it a high-tech **throwback** to a time when perishable foods were delivered to customers by horse-drawn wagons.

Prospects and Perils

Why are automakers and others investing billions of dollars in self-driving cars? The primary reason is safety. About 40,000 people— drivers, passengers, bicyclists, and pedestrians—die in U.S. traffic accidents every year. Many more suffer serious injuries. Authorities believe that the majority of these accidents are caused by driver error. Advocates of self-driving cars believe that removing drivers will make roads

OPPOSITE: Before self-driving cars are available for general use, they will need to go through many hours of testing and training about how to react to cars driven by humans.

safer for everyone. Many reasons for deadly accidents will simply vanish. More than one-third of crashes involve drunk drivers. Self-driving cars will never consume alcohol. Many accidents are a result of texting or other distractions while driving. Self-driving cars won't be distracted. And they won't fall asleep while on the road—thereby eliminating yet another major cause of accidents. These accidents cost the economy nearly $50 billion every year.

Many people believe that vast fleets of self-driving cars will largely replace individual car ownership. The majority of people will use a simple app to summon a ride whenever it is needed. According to estimates, people spend nearly $10,000 every year on their vehicles: monthly loan payments, fuel, insurance, and ever-increasing maintenance. The price of the app would be far less,

According to estimates, people spend nearly $10,000 every year on their vehicles: monthly loan payments, fuel, insurance, and ever-increasing maintenance.

thereby saving several thousands of dollars for those who give up their cars. There's another advantage. To earn a driver's license, individuals have to learn how to drive. This process has a steep learning curve. Self-driving cars are all preprogrammed with the latest improvements when they begin operations.

Most vehicles in use today depend on the internal combustion engine. These vehicles release gases that pollute the atmosphere. When they're not in use, they sit idly—as much as 95 percent of the time. They occupy significant space in parking lots, at home, in shopping

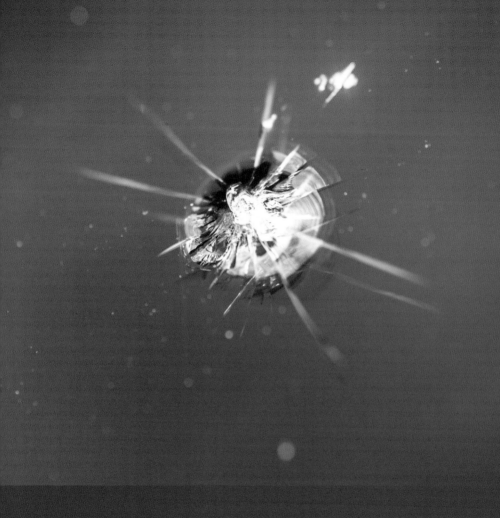

High Tech

In most cases, if a flying pebble creates a small crack in a car's windshield, it can be filled and repaired. But the windshield is a vital part of self-driving cars. Features such as automatic emergency braking systems rely on windshield-mounted cameras. If a new windshield isn't precisely **calibrated**, the cameras may focus too far down the road. This would cause the car to slam on its brakes. A calibration may need to be done in a specially equipped garage. It may also require extensive on-road testing. Both add extra time and cost to the repair bill. By 2022, automatic emergency braking systems will be standard equipment on most new vehicles. As cars edge closer to full autonomy, windshields will become even more complex.

malls, and at sports arenas. Most experts envision that self-driving cars will be electrically powered and in continuous operation—providing solutions to both of these problems.

Americans in urban areas spend an average of 42 hours a year sitting in traffic while getting to and from work. In Boston, drivers suffer through more than 160 hours of traffic jams every year. Self-driving cars are likely to operate more efficiently. Also, there will potentially be fewer of them on the roads, a combination

that will significantly reduce congestion.

Self-driving cars could have a huge effect on healthcare. Nearly 4 million Americans miss or put off medical appointments each year because they lack access to transportation. These missed appointments create significant issues for healthcare providers and drive up medical costs. Self-driving vehicles would make it far easier to keep appointments by picking up patients at home.

While the primary emphasis of self-driving vehicles is on human transportation, the technology has other applications. Self-driving vehicles could help farmers perform the seemingly endless drudgery of planting their crops and then harvesting them. Construction sites could benefit from a stream of self-driving trucks lining up to take on loads of excavated dirt and then dumping it elsewhere, rather than using a human driver who spends

A 2018 study showed that nearly 75 percent of drivers would be afraid to give up control.

much of the workday sitting around. Long-haul truckers could turn over control of their rigs to a computer. This would reduce the strain associated with driving for long periods of time.

But there are issues with self-driving cars. They do well in sunny climates where lane lines are always visible. But snow and debris on the roadway obscures those lines. Cameras sometimes have a hard time penetrating heavy rain or fog. Radar can detect potential obstacles but can't show their shapes. The computer may not be sure how to respond to these unknown obstacles. Lidar can be fooled by snowflakes. The light beams bounce off them and interpret them as obstacles.

Consumer acceptance is another issue. People are so accustomed to being in charge of their vehicles that they will likely resist turning over control to a computer. A 2018 study showed that nearly 75 percent of drivers would be afraid to give up control.

There are several reasons why many people would still want to own their own vehicle rather than share an autonomous service. Just like the Ford Model T more than a century ago, mass production of these cars will lower the price. According to some estimates, the cost

may drop to as little as $10,000. That is far lower than most new cars today. In addition, keeping personal belongings in a car is convenient. This is especially true of parents of young children who keep car seats in the car. Commuters would enjoy the luxury of doing work in what is effectually a small office if they have their own vehicles. An especially important consideration is that the time to summon a car in densely packed urban areas is just a few minutes. Longer waits could be the rule in more distant suburbs and even more so in rural areas.

Sadly, the first known U.S. fatality involving a self-driving car occurred in Florida in May 2016. A truck made a left turn in front of the car, killing its driver. The National Transportation Safety Board concluded that the system functioned properly, and blamed the accident on driver error. Another fatality occurred in Tempe,

Arizona, two years later. A self-driving car ran over a pedestrian. People were angry. A man slashed the tire of a self-driving vehicle at a stoplight. Another man pulled alongside a vehicle and used physical force to threaten the occupant. In another instance, a man threatened an employee with a .22 caliber pistol. Yet another man drove head-on toward a self-driving car, forcing it to screech to a stop. He told police that his son had nearly been hit while playing. "There are other places they can test," he said. "They said they need real-world examples, but I don't want to be their real-world mistake." Self-driving vehicles won't replace humans overnight. It could take years, or even decades. During that time, self-driving cars will have to share the road with humans who often act unpredictably.

The Road Ahead

One of the biggest concerns about self-driving cars is the potential for major job losses. According to estimates, more than 3 million current jobs could be eliminated by self-driving vehicles. Rideshare and taxi drivers, truckers, and delivery van operators all could find themselves out of work. These concerns may be exaggerated. "The net impact of automation on employment has always been a positive, rather than a

OPPOSITE: A transition to driverless vehicles could change the way roads, intersections, and interstate highway systems are designed and developed.

Many people feared that ATMs would eliminate bank tellers when they were introduced in the 1970s and 1980s.

negative, economy-wide," said John Paul MacDuffie, director of the University of Pennsylvania's Wharton School of Business program on vehicle and mobility innovation. "There's no reason to expect that this time will be any different."

The experience with automatic teller machines (ATMs) provides an example. Many people feared that ATMs would eliminate bank tellers when they were introduced in the 1970s and 1980s. The opposite happened. Banks established many new branch offices. While each branch needed fewer tellers than previously, there were so many new ones that the total number of tellers actually increased.

In many cases, workers have transitioned almost seamlessly from a suddenly outdated technology to a new one. For example, a Massachusetts family business began in the 19th century with the blacksmith trade. When motorized vehicles replaced the horse-drawn carriage, the business adapted to the new transportation environment. It continues to adapt. "It was a big deal back in the 1990s when we bought our first computer; now there are computers all over the shop," said the current owner. "The technology is screaming forward."

Something similar may happen with self-driving cars. While they will undoubtedly take away some jobs, many people believe they will create even more. For example, taxi drivers could take on new roles with their vehicles, transitioning from doing the actual driving to assisting

passengers, especially seniors and children. Such jobs would not require significant education or training. Other jobs might involve keeping the cars in tip-top cosmetic condition, such as washing the outside and cleaning the inside—especially if someone gets sick in the vehicle.

On-demand delivery services using self-driving vehicles are poised to become popular. Since there will be no need to pay drivers, the overall cost of the service will be lower, thereby increasing demand and helping to create jobs in maintaining the vehicles, keeping them stocked with food or merchandise, and dealing with customer calls. Companies such as FedEx and Amazon are also experimenting with autonomous delivery methods such as bots and drones.

Many additional jobs will come from startups that will want to take advantage of the interest in self-driving

World of Carcraft

Waymo invented a virtual software system to test its self-driving cars. Because many people working on the project have played the popular video game *World of Warcraft*, the company named this system Carcraft. It has virtual re-creations of cities in various parts of the U.S. Every day, the software's fleet of 25,000 virtual cars drive up to 8 million miles in these "cities." In comparison, Waymo's real-life cars cover about 3 million miles on public roads. Carcraft puts particular emphasis on tricky road conditions. Especially difficult situations may be tested several hundred times in a single day. The next step is using this data to improve actual self-driving cars for operating in the real world.

Aurora is a new company that develops software for self-driving cars. It went from 3 people at its founding in 2017 to more than 200 in less than 2 years.

cars. These startups often demonstrate explosive growth. For example, Aurora is a new company that develops software for self-driving cars. It went from 3 people at its founding in 2017 to more than 200 in less than 2 years. Zoox, which is designing its own self-driving car, went from 4 people in 2014 to more than 500 in 2018. Many more companies are experiencing similar growth. None is showing any signs of a slowdown as they attract significant investments.

Even the loss of truck-driving jobs may not be as severe as some people think. "Navigating the terminals and roads leading to interstates will require a lot of

PICTURED Autonomous vehicles use sensors to detect traffic, signposts, and lane lines on roads, but weather conditions like rain or snow can interfere with their performance.

driver interaction for quite some time to come; drivers also have a lot of interaction with their cargo," said a FedEx official. "Once you get on the highway, where driving can be a monotonous task, we think automated vehicles have the potential to take over, improving safety and driver quality of life." Drivers could perform other tasks, such as bookkeeping and inventory management. They could even relax, take a nap, read, or watch videos. These perks might make the profession more appealing to younger people.

Unsurprisingly, the development and growth of self-driving vehicles has created many openings for software engineers and similar positions. By mid-2018, online postings for these jobs had increased by more than 25 percent from the start of the year. Most of these new positions require a college education. In schools today,

Andrew Moore, the dean of CMU's School of Computer Science, recently claimed that graduates with robotics engineering skills can command salaries of up to $200,000.

there is an increasing emphasis on STEM (science, technology, engineering, and mathematics) education. It can lead to countless numbers of high-paying jobs. Self-driving cars are no exception. For example, Andrew Moore, the dean of CMU's School of Computer Science, recently claimed that graduates with robotics engineering skills can command salaries of up to $200,000. That is "unheard of for any role until recently," he added.

Self-driving vehicle companies will also need employees who have qualified technical skills. Mechanics are needed to keep the cars in good running order.

Not-so-free Parking

Ridesharing is one way self-driving cars could cut down on the total number of vehicles on the road. But this could come at a cost. When people drive somewhere, they must find a parking place. Often this is in pay lots or on city streets with parking meters. But self-driving cars might not need to park after dropping off passengers. While waiting for their next pickup, they may cruise at a low speed rather than parking. "Even when you factor in electricity, **depreciation**, wear and tear, and maintenance, cruising costs about 50 cents an hour—that's cheaper than parking, even in a small town," said transportation planner Adam Millard-Ball. Low-speed cruising could double the number of vehicles in urban areas.

These jobs will entail customary work such as routine maintenance, oil changes (for non-electric vehicles), and tire replacement. Existing and new mechanics will require additional technical training to be able to service important components such as lidar sensors. Dispatchers are another important area. These personnel will have to know where the cars are at any moment and send them to meet customers. A third area is fleet response. If vehicles encounter unexpected obstacles, such as fallen trees in the roadway, the response team will provide an alternate route. Customer service representatives will be needed to deal with passenger questions and complaints. By tapping on a button, riders will be in touch with them to ask whatever questions may arise, ranging from how to plug in music devices to dealing with emergencies. And for people who would otherwise be housebound because of

an inability to drive, easy access to autonomous vehicles could open up millions of jobs for them.

In just a few years, self-driving vehicles have gone from existing only in sci-fi stories to driving on real roads. At some point, they might take care of all of our transportation needs. It is certainly an exciting time to be in the automobile industry or related fields.

Timeline

1925   Inventor Francis Houdina's *American Wonder* travels the streets of Manhattan without a driver.

1935   David Keller's short story "The Living Machine" features driverless cars.

1939   GM showcases a driverless future in its Futurama Exhibit at the 1939 World's Fair in New York City.

1955   Computer scientist John McCarthy coins the term "artificial intelligence."

1984   Carnegie Mellon University (CMU) develops the Terragator, a primitive self-driving car.

1986   CMU begins the NavLab series of self-driving cars.

1995   CMU researchers embark on the "No Hands Across America" trip, with an on-board computer controlling nearly all the driving.

2004   The DARPA Grand Challenge creates interest in self-driving cars, but none of the teams finishes.

2005   Five vehicles finish the course in the second DARPA Grand Challenge.

2007   DARPA Urban Challenge involves a 55-mile (88.5 km) course in a simulated urban setting.

2009   The Google Self-Driving Car Project begins.

2013   Elon Musk announces that Tesla will develop a self-driving car.

2016   The Google unit responsible for driverless car
       development is renamed Waymo and becomes a
       separate company.

2018   Waymo vehicles log a combined 10 million miles' worth
       of driving.

2019   Waymo announces plans for a factory in Michigan—the
       first solely devoted to self-driving cars.

Selected Bibliography

Agrawal, Ajay, Joshua Gans, and Avi Goldfarb. *Prediction Machines: The Simple Economics of Artificial Intelligence.* Boston: Harvard Business Review Press, 2018.

Burns, Lawrence D., and Christopher Shulgan. *Autonomy: The Quest to Build the Driverless Car—And How It Will Reshape Our World.* New York: HarperCollins, 2018.

Davies, Alex. "How Do Self-Driving Cars See?" *Wired.* November 8, 2018. https://www.wired.com/story/the-know-it-alls-how-do-self-driving-cars-see/.

Dormehl, Luke, and Stephen Edelstein. "10 Major Milestones in the History of Self-Driving Cars." *Digital Trends.* February 2, 2019. https://www.digitaltrends.com/cars/history-of-self-driving-cars-milestones/.

Herrmann, Andreas, Walter Brenner, and Rupert Stadler. *Autonomous Driving: How the Driverless Revolution Will Change the World.* Bingley, U.K.: Emerald, 2018.

Husain, Amir. *The Sentient Machine: The Coming Age of Artificial Intelligence.* New York: Scribner, 2017.

Lipson, Hod, and Melba Kurman. *Driverless: Intelligent Cars and the Road Ahead.* Cambridge, Mass.: MIT Press, 2016.

Glossary

advocates people who support something and speak out in favor of it

autonomous undertaken without outside control; self-contained or independent

behemoth something huge or enormous

calibrated carefully adjusted

circuitry detailed plan of electrical circuits

depreciation reduction of value over a period of time

entrepreneur a person who organizes and develops a somewhat risky business

Global Positioning System a system of satellites, computers, and other electronic devices that work together to determine the location of objects or living things that carry a trackable device

hairpin a sharp, U-shaped curve in a roadway

Internet domain name registry database of domain names and information regarding the registrant associated with the name

laser a device that produces a concentrated beam of light

phantom a ghost

radar   a system used to detect objects and
                  determine their position and velocity

scale model   a test version of an object that is uniformly
                  reduced or enlarged to be in proportion to
                  the surroundings

throwback   going back to an earlier time period

underpinnings foundations, supports

Websites

Computer History Museum
*https://www.computerhistory.org/atchm/where-to-a-history-of
-autonomous-vehicles/*

Discover more about the history of self-driving vehicles
through text and pictures.

The Drive
*https://www.thedrive.com/sheetmetal/16916/lidar-vs-radar
-pros-and-cons-of-different-autonomous-driving-technologies*

Watch video clips to learn more about how autonomous
vehicles operate with lidar.

Note: Every effort has been made to ensure that any websites listed above were
active at the time of publication. However, because of the nature of the Internet, it is
impossible to guarantee that these sites will remain active indefinitely or that their
contents will not be altered.

Index